THE RAW
STILLNESS
OF HEAVEN

TIM BETE

www.GrayRising.com

ISBN-13: 978-1542803946
ISBN-10: 1542803942

Available in print and e-book
on Amazon.com.

This collection of poems is dedicated
to all who search for God.
May you find Him in holy silence.

TABLE OF CONTENTS

Beginnings

Prayer

Conversion

Faith

Endings

BEGINNINGS

"The feeling remains that God
is on the journey, too."

— Saint Teresa of Avila

Dear Lucy —

A little food for "the space inside" you.

With love always

Rachel x
x

5 a.m. Prayer

The fog of sleep
gives way to the fog of faith,

prayer intentions wafting
in a murky mist—

curling around
suffering and doubt;

pleas drifting
through time and space.

How are feeble petitions
rendered into God's velvet

breath? Slowly they creep
under locked doors,

until sacred dew descends,
quenching all.

In the Beginning

God created time
so I could travel to a day

when I love Him more
than I love myself.

Decades bound together
with sinews of grace;

years ticking, seasons
pulling me along,

like a mother on a mission—
holding her toddler's hand,

not allowing the child
to linger nor run ahead

until the destination's reached.
Yet in each moment,

an opportunity to change mind
or heart or will. Each body

a time machine—a gift
not even the angels possess.

Hanger Shirts

Each year before school started, mother led
him to the store, through the men's department,

past the boys' clothing to the back room
with the faded cardboard sign that said:

Irregulars.

He didn't know what made him irregular—
perhaps it was the birthmark on his left leg

or the cowlick of hair he had to smash down
with water each morning before the bus came.

Heaps of clothing lay tangled in large gray bins,
not possessing the common courtesy to line up

for easy inspection on wooden hangers.
Some pieces tried to escape over the bin edges

and onto the floor, as if not even the shirts
and pants wanted to associate with him.

His mother plunged her arms deep
into piles of cloth, like a scuba diver hunting

for sunken treasure, trying to find a pearl
that had gone undetected by other shoppers.

As she grumbled, "awful button holes"
and "horrible seam stitching,"

he anxiously raised his eyes to see
if any of the other customers had noticed

he was irregular—the sign suspended
from the ceiling like a lighthouse beacon,

warning the richer families to stay away.
He knew it was too much to wish

for a hanger shirt: a shirt neatly pressed
and arranged by size on a shiny metal rack.

He had once asked his mother about hanger shirts
but she had just shot him a look he knew meant

he should be quiet and forget that question.
Standing in front of the clothing bin, his head

bowed, all thought of hope and hangers
slipped away until a pair of pants hit him

in the ribs, pressing his pendant Crucifix
into his chest—the form of one irregular boy

leaving its impression on another. And he heard
his mother say, "Try those on in the fitting room."

Where God Hides

Between the inhale and the exhale
lies a house where God dwells.

He rests in the lull after
the prayer and before the amen,

and curls up in the darkness
between the match strike and the flame.

He reclines in the crevice
made by gently-held hands

as well as in the instant
between eye-close and kiss.

Sometimes He hides in the furrows
among ripples on a pond

or in the head of a candle snuffer—
yellow glow turned to smoke.

Even a ubiquitous God
has His favorite hiding places

where He prefers to spend time
while he's also everywhere else.

First Words

Small, soft clouds drift
from the newborn's lips,

mingling with vapor
from the mouths

of mother and father,
donkeys and cows,

as well as steam
from dung piles.

Small, soft clouds
longed-for by priests

and publicans,
wise men and widows,

saints and sinners.
What would this newborn

say if he could talk?
He would say,

"Today you will be
with me in paradise."

The Raw Stillness of Heaven

How is it that your poem
bridges the chasm
from God to my soul?

As water primes a pump,
your words bring forth a prayer
that slakes my heart.

Words I didn't know
were mine until you
put them into my mouth.

Your pen punctures
the raw stillness of Heaven,
love spilling out like chrism,

anointing my head and ears,
my eyes and lips.
Each stanza is a sacrament,

ink mingling with holy silence
to form a new incarnation.
As God meets your hand,

somehow grace is captured
on a flimsy page, connecting
me once again to my Lord.

PRAYER

"For me, prayer is a surge of the heart;
it is a simple look turned toward heaven..."

— St. Therese of Lisieux

Silent Winter Prayer

The stippled sky was a tabernacle,
moon glowing like a sanctuary lamp,

the smell of melting wax and incense
replaced by pine and cold air.

The dirt road was covered by snow
crunching under foot, breaking

the stillness: until I stopped. Motionless,
ears cocked, there was no sound

except darkness and silent peace—
the world's vastness frozen in time.

At that moment, You pierced my heart,
fracturing the tabernacle of the woods,

making the stars more radiant, the moon
sharper, as I stood in awe alone with You.

On that journey home, across the frozen pond,
You stayed with me, rending my heart

until I knew there was no other reason
for living except to be with You.

Litany of the Wind Farm

An hour and a half into the drive
from Indianapolis to Chicago
begins the litany of alabaster arms.

God is with you,
God is with you,
God is with you.

White dots sprouting into giants;
feet rooted, they dance–
strident voices demanding an answer.

Have you seen Him,
Have you seen Him,
Have you seen Him?

Synchronized swimmers
that slice the sky
before slashing the grain.

He is waiting,
He is waiting,
He is waiting.

Slowly they sink away,
gusty voices fading,
yet their prayer remains.

St. Dominic's Patio Chair

I have spent hundreds of hours
praying in the blue patio chair
in my office—across from the bookcase

filled with rolls of duct tape and fishing
gear and a tub of spackling paste. Plastic
mesh pulled tight between powder-coated

metal arms and legs—arms just far enough
apart so my elbows don't touch them
when my hands are folded in my lap.

Hands lie nestled one inside the other,
fingers never intertwined; bare feet
shifting back and forth on the carpet

like grazing animals, until they find
their perfect spot. Is it a paradox
to find my sweet Lord's presence

in a place designed for drinking beer
between games of cornhole? I wonder
if the chair misses its compatriots, exiled

outside in the rain around the umbrella
table. Perhaps it is they who think
the indoor chair has been exiled.

St. Dominic surely would have included
my chair in his nine ways of prayer,
had he sat in it for only a few minutes—

inserting the chair sitting position between
standing erect with arms outstretched
and reaching towards heaven like an arrow.

When I get to Heaven and find
a place prepared for me, I hope
that place has a blue patio chair,

for there are times when I imagine
worshiping God for all eternity
sitting in this chair. And I hope

in Heaven, I meet St. Dominic
so he can try my chair and comment
how comfortable it is and how his

elbows don't touch the arms, as I watch
his feet graze the floor before settling in.
But for today, the chair and the bookcase

and the rain outside are mine, as I sit
with the Lord, my soul resting
in a chair disposed to prayer.

The Pilgrimage

For a dozen hours I rode on a bus
with 32 high schoolers to see
Pope Francis, our decades of the Rosary
interspersed with Disney movies.

A strange thing, listening on my earbuds
to Benedictine nuns and Dominican sisters
chanting *Duo Seraphim* and *Christe Sanctorum*
while watching images from *Tangled*

and *High School Musical*—Gabriella and Troy
attempting to discover if they were meant
for each other. But perhaps no stranger
than watching teenagers embrace life

with an enthusiasm I envy and an outpouring
of love that reveals they grasp their faith
much better than I imagined. Some might
call them the future of the Church

but it seems to me they are the Church
of today as much as anyone—
accepting of God's grace and each other—
unsure what is ahead but willing to rely

on God's providence as they share their lunches
with the homeless—arms intertwined,
dancing through the streets of Philadelphia,
on a pilgrimage to see Pope Francis.

Baking God

She brushes a spot of flour
off the collar of her shirt
before removing a sandwich
from a paper bag and pouring

black coffee into a cup—
a break from her job filling
vats with wheat and water.
Each day she inspects

small circles of bread
destined to become God—
thankful for paid contemplation;
the factory, her convent;

production line, her cell;
denim shirt, her habit;
machines whirr-click-clacking,
filling the air like monastic chant.

Breathless

Sometimes when I work,
I forget You, focusing

on the task at hand,
while You sneak up on me—

and with a single breath,
You leave me breathless.

Startled by Your certainty,
a wisp kindling a flame,

You revive my soul,
and I know You are here.

Sometimes while I work,
I can feel Your verse,

the cadence of my Lord;
poetry in my heart.

As each line unwinds,
another ember is added,

Your words searing within,
and I know You are here.

Sometimes while I work,
there is only silence,

no poem, no breath, no voice—
no sign of You at all.

Yet even in this dark,
simply thinking of You

is enough to know
You are here,

just the thought of You,
leaving me breathless.

Unless

Like stacked bales of wool,
walls of silence form a barricade,
keeping me safely within my cell—

unless they block my way,
banishing me to the outside, alone
with only a hunger to be within.

CONVERSION

"We shall never learn to know ourselves
except by endeavoring to know God;
for, beholding His greatness, we realize
our own littleness; His purity
shows us our foulness..."

— Saint Teresa of Avila

The Stench

They abandoned their boats and nets
along with activities of past lives,
attachments discarded like rotting fish
left to stink and decay.

You duped me Lord, granting
my greedy ambition, then making
me nauseous at its sight, the mere
thought repulsive to my heart.

What I so eagerly sought
became a maggot-filled carcass,
causing me to retch, unable
to gulp a fresh breath while

wading through the heavy fumes
at the edge of faith's shore.
Desperate, like Peter, to follow You
and leave behind the vomitous

stench of sin—praying
that like Peter's net, my soul
would begin to tear under
the immense weight of Your love.

Man on Fire

If I could truly see my sin,
would I shrivel up and die

or dive into the waters of God's love,
like a man on fire?

Does sin run out behind me,
like a basket of sand on my back,

pouring through the cracks,
easy for others to see,

while invisible to me?
I pray to clearly see my sin,

then quickly pray it remain
hidden; uncertain if the sight

would kill me or drive me
again into His arms.

Confessional Line

Waiting in patient queue
to trade actions

that make me cringe
for forgiveness.

Not an even trade—
sin for grace—

an exorbitant exchange
made possible by God

through a small
confessional window.

Each time, I firmly intend
to sin no more and avoid

whatever leads to sin,
yet I know I will be back,

aching to hear Him say,
"I grant you pardon

and peace and absolve
you of your sins,"

so I can pick up my stretcher
and go home.

Groundhog Day

Between the dark paneled walls
of the confessional box,
I often feel like Bill Murray
in the movie, *Groundhog Day*–

living the same 24 hours
over and over again;
praying to wake up
without hearing

I've Got You Babe
on the radio or bumping
into Ned Ryerson
on the street corner.

I long for dreary sin
to cease, the endless
time loop to expire;
yearning for today

to become tomorrow,
the ritual complete–
a final purification
filled with peace and mercy.

The Longest Road

How many days did he walk,
mulling over words he would say
to a father scorned and insulted?
Replaying scenarios in his mind.

Still so focused on himself
all he could think of was,
"I will say this and he
will probably say that."

Reliving each burning memory.
Scourging himself for past deeds.
Recreating pain and misery.
Kindling the blaze of a private Hell.

And if for a moment he considered
forgiveness, he quickly threw fuel
on his pain until it exploded
with all thought of mercy consumed.

At home, a father's love burned.
Thinking only of his son's return,
not a second spent on past deeds—
the fire of hope sustained him.

A father filled with the
cremating blaze of compassion,
turning all memories of sin
forever into ash.

When they met on the road:
an embrace, a kiss, an apology unheard—
their two fires collided,
one of pain, the other of love,

and at that moment
the son could not remember
why he had left; nor could he fathom
the thought of ever leaving again.

FAITH

"If a man wishes to be sure of the road
he's traveling on, then he must close
his eyes and travel in the dark."

— St. John of the Cross

One Thing Remained

Thumbs pressed firmly on his eyelids,
fingers wrapped over his ears,
while the crowd rustled and murmured
amid the sweat and dust.

Why had he answered, "yes," when asked,
"Do you believe I can do this?"
He didn't know if he really believed
or simply had a desperate longing—

if there was even a difference
between the two. For seventeen years
he had grasped at straws; deceived
by both physicians and Pharisees.

When the stranger said, "Let it be
done for you according to your faith,"
the man wondered if it was mercy
or if he was being mocked for his lack

of conviction; having so often been taunted.
Memories swelled—dreams of the torrent
of light that might again fill his body.
With eyes still shut, he feared hope—

as the years had taught him to fear it.
Yet only one thing remained: To open
with even the smallest scrap of trust,
expecting brilliant blaze or enduring night.

Repayment

What will God find when He looks
within, searching a soul emptied
to make a dwelling place for Him?

He will see Himself, for that is all
my soul can hold. And when He sees
Himself, rejoicing at the Love He's found—

a Love that is also Him—how is it He
will repay me, who am neither the seeker
nor the Love, but only the container

in which He dwells? Without His blood,
a chalice is only a cup; without His body,
a tabernacle just a box. He creates

and sustains all I am and yet it is He
who repays me—a strange repayment
of that which was never first given.

The Thirteen

Behind St. Joseph's walls, thirteen began,
hidden from the world while saving it,
hands raised in prayer, God heard them
and gave them the better of the fight.

Behind closed doors, thirteen began,
knowing God that He might be known,
detached from those outside
that those outside might be attached to Him.

Within their cells, thirteen began,
patiently searching for the Lord,
sacrificing all for Him who is all,
giving in to His will at every turn.

Within their souls, thirteen began,
conversing with their Lord,
climbing to the top of His mountain,
loving only Him; only Him.

Behind St. Joseph's walls, thirteen began,
their prayer spreading around the world
until thirteen became thousands,
conquering the world through silence.

Mystery

With each insight You grant,
Your mystery grows larger
until I know much more
and yet much less about You.

Love's enigma erases
the questions my mind once asked.
Being with You is enough—
in silence is Your love.

Beholden

I tell you a mystery
of the heavens high above,
of the angel of the Lord
and the virgin with child.

Behold, the blessed handmaid,
the magi from the east,
the day of salvation,
the man; our King has come!

Behold, He dwells with us,
making all things new,
He casts out demons
and heals the sick.

Behold, He proclaims good news,
unlocking the Heavens,
He desires sincerity
and has left an open door.

Behold, the Bridegroom
and the banquet.
Behold, His hour, as He is
handed over to sinners.

Behold, the Lamb of God
and the hand of the betrayer,
the great earthquake,
the torn veil of the sanctuary.

Behold, the place He was lain
and two in dazzling garments,
His coming in the clouds
and the kingdom of God.

Behold, I tell you a mystery,
I owe all to His grace, for He
has made me both beholder
and beholden.

The Bishop of Billings Street

Like an ancient fleshy monument
he sits on a faded plastic cathedra,
two small dogs orbiting around him.
Barking acolytes on a grass altar.

Raising an arm,
he blesses me as I pass,
grunting "henh,"
which I know from experience

means "how are you today"
or "I'm glad you noticed me"
or "I will be here tomorrow
because I have no place else to be."

In Summer, quart beer bottle in hand,
he absolves cars and squirrels
as well as the occasional homeless man
rummaging through his garbage can.

In Fall, incense-like ribbons from his cigar
purify school bus pick-ups and drop-offs,
punctuated by the arrival of his home-care aide
who makes his lunch each day at 11:45.

In Winter, his chair stands alone,
alternately covered in snow and ice,
his dogs still orbiting around it
when they go outside to do their business.

Each Spring, I await
his awakening, his hibernation
complete. Like Lazarus
abandoning the tomb, he rises.

Screen door slamming behind him
he limps back to his place in the yard,
wielding his cane like a crozier,
to once again pray over his flock.

I Dreamed a Dream

that at His feet I knelt
as He lay on the cross,

hands already pierced,
feet not yet driven through.

His face I couldn't see—
only His legs and feet

but I could hear his pain
and anticipation

that His feet were next.
"Oh Lord," I wept,

"My Lord, oh Lord, my Lord,"
Nothing else could I say but

"My Lord, oh Lord, my Lord."
As my tears fell onto unpierced feet,

"My Lord, oh Lord, my Lord,"
feet I kissed again and again,

"My Lord, oh Lord, my Lord."
And in my dream, I don't why,

"My Lord, oh Lord, my Lord,"
my tears of sorrow eased His pain,

"My Lord, oh Lord, my Lord,"
as my chest convulsed, I sobbed,

"My Lord, oh Lord, my Lord,"
until the soldiers pushed me away,

"My Lord, oh Lord, my Lord,"
and made His feet as were His hands.

Endings

"The world's thy ship
and not thy home."

— St. Therese of Lisieux

Invocation for a Dying Man

How we prayed.
Our pleas rose
like a bird that spies

a piece of silver foil
and enamored with its sheen,
carries it to its nest,

thinking it an incredible
treasure—until it fades
in the sun and rain.

God took the man
and we sobbed because
God hadn't listened.

Yet we had asked for a miracle
and one had been granted—
concealed from our view,

the man's pain transformed
into paradise and his faults
washed with endless love.

Unknown Martyr

Each night, she scrubs tile floors
after waiting tables all day:
her hands and knees raw, exhaustion
bringing her one day closer to death.

Her only thought, a son and daughter—
how to keep them fed with a roof over head,
how to survive another month,
how to pray in the midst of pain.

Kneeling on dirty, wet vestibule block
is not as glamorous as Joan (burnt by soldiers)
or Clement (tossed with an anchor into the sea)
or Stephen (stoned by a mob).

Each Saint quickly sacrificed
while her martyrdom is decades long,
her life laid down bit by bit each evening
through the instrument of a soapy brush.

Love's Call

I do not long for death,
though I was born to die.

Each day, closer I creep
toward my union with Love.

I'm very like my Love,
who, too, was born to die.

Yet death He nimbly smashed,
like a fragile earthen vase

and called out to His souls,
"come through this death to Me."

I hear Him call my name,
bright silence in my soul.

For Him and Him alone,
a bit more falls each day.

I do not long for death,
though I was born to die.

Gray Rising

Dimly-lit church, empty
except for the strong lingering scent

of spicy-sweet smoke
from a funeral earlier in the day.

Gray rising clouds
no longer visible,

stale recollections left behind
with memories of a soul I did not know.

Lives sputter and ignite
like aromatic crystals

heaped onto blistering coals,
souls billowing and ascending.

Nine Miles Outside Yakima

He was thinking about home
when the grenade
bounced into the foxhole—
and for a split second
he thought it looked like
a pear from the orchard
at his family's farm,
nine miles outside Yakima.

He imagined the fragrance
of the budding pear trees
and the wind sifting
through the leaves, as he
threw his body down
to smother the fruit,
compelled by an instinct
he hadn't known he possessed.

Inches in front of him
stood his Sergeant's boots—
the same color as the ones
his father wore on the farm—
eyes frantically scanning up
Sarge's pant leg, hoping to reach
his face, desperate for reassurance
the moment wasn't real.

When the chaplain drove up
the long dirt driveway, he saw
the mother hanging laundry
in the side yard. Dropping a sheet
to the ground, she stared—
her gaze straining to push
the car away; tears falling before
the chaplain closed the car door.

They buried their son on the hill
with a view of the pear trees
and the back porch—where
in the evenings he used to drink
iced tea—on the porch where he
had first told them he'd enlisted,
with no thought of foxholes or grenades,
nine miles outside Yakima.

God Whispers

When I told you My love was so great
that I wanted to spend eternity with you,

I didn't mean an eternity at some far-off time,
as if everlasting life was a clock wound

by your death. Eternity began the day
I conceived your soul—on that day,

I unfurled within you, long before your birth;
long before you first saw the world.

Yet you forget our eternity is well underway,
squandering our time as you imagine me

in some far-off place, aloof and hidden.
From your conception, no time will ever separate us;

not a second of your earthly life or thereafter.
You always have been and always will be

Mine.

NOTES

A few thoughts on some of the poems in this collection...

First Words
While they were both hanging on crosses, Jesus said to the good thief, "Today you will be with me in Paradise" (Luke 23:43). I've often thought that is something Jesus says to us every day of our lives.

The Raw Stillness of Heaven
One of St. Teresa of Avila's poems inspired this response. In her poem she wrote the line, "I die because I do not die," which, for me, sums up the spiritual life.

St. Dominic's Patio Chair
There is a framed print of St. Dominic's Nine Ways of Prayer at the Motherhouse of the Dominican Sisters of Mary, Mother of the Eucharist, where our daughter is a Dominican Sister. I've often admired the print, as well as St. Dominic.

Baking God
I realize when communion bread is made, it is more of a waffle iron approach than baking, but baking just seems more like God to me.

The Stench
As a boy, I fished on the Connecticut River during the annual shad spawning run. Many of the large fish would end up stranded on rocks in the sun, causing one of the worst smells I have ever experienced. If sin has a smell, it's dead shad.

Confessional Line
"Pick up my stretcher" is a reference to Mark 2:11, where Jesus tells the paralytic to pick up his mat and go home.

Groundhog Day
The movie, *Groundhog Day*, is often included in lists of the best Catholic movies and it's one of my favorites. (By the way, Bill Murray is Catholic.)

The Longest Road
This poem was inspired by the parable of the prodigal son (Luke 15:11) as well as by the famous painting by Rembrandt.

One Thing Remained
I've often wondered what was going through the minds of those healed by Jesus. This poem is a reflection on Matthew 9:27.

Repayment
Matthew 6:4 says, "your Father who sees in secret will repay you." It always seemed like an odd thing that God would repay me since He has given me everything I have and am.

The Thirteen
St. Teresa of Avila's first foundation (convent) was named St. Joseph. Thirteen Carmelite nuns lived there. The line "...hands raised in prayer, God heard them and gave them the better of the fight" is a

reference to Exodus 17:11, in which Israel had the better of the fight as long as Moses kept his hands raised. As a Secular Carmelite, I have a special devotion to St. Teresa.

Beholden

A *cento* is a poem made up of lines from other poems. This poem is a modified cento, with each line except the last four coming from Scripture in which the word "behold" is used. The Scripture verses are:

1 Corinthians 15:51
Job 35:5
Matthew 2:13
Matthew 1:23

Luke 1:38
Matthew 2:1
2 Corinthians 6:2
John 19:5; John 19:14

Revelation 21:3
Revelation 21:5
Luke 13:32
Luke 13:32

Luke 2:10
Matthew 3:16
Psalms 51:8
Revelation 3:8

Matthew 25:6
Matthew 22:4
John 16:32
Mark 14:41

John 1:29
Luke 22:21
Matthew 28:2
Matthew 27:51

Mark 16:6
Luke 24:4
Revelation 1:7
Luke 17:21

I Dreamed a Dream
This poem is based on an actual dream. It is the only time in my life I can remember waking in tears.

Unknown Martyr
St. Joan of Arc was burned at the stake. St. Clement of Rome (Pope Clement I) was tossed into the sea with an anchor around his neck. St. Stephen was stoned to death (Acts 6).

Nines Miles Outside Yakima
I've never been to Yakima, Washington, except in my mind while writing this poem.

ABOUT THE AUTHOR

While Tim Bete has been a writer for much of his life, he only started writing poetry after he entered his fifties and began spending a significant amount of time in silent prayer. The more time he spent in silence, the greater the ease he had writing poetry. In a way, Tim's poems are his prayer journal.

Tim is a member of the Secular Order of Discalced Carmelites and often trades poems with his oldest daughter, who is a Dominican Sister. (He says she is the best writer in the family.)

Tim is the author of *In the Beginning...There Were No Diapers*, a book of essays on the mysteries of parenting (Ave Maria Press). His writing has appeared in several editions of the *Amazing Grace* anthology series (Ascension Press), the *Christian Science Monitor*, the *Poet and Contemplative Blog* of the Discalced Carmelite Friars (Province of St. Therese), as well as CatholicLane.com and other Websites. *The Raw Stillness of Heaven* is his first book of poetry.

More of Tim's poetry can be found at
www.GrayRising.com.